Bibliology Booklet

Bibliology Booklet

Bibliology® Press

Weimar, California

Bibliology Booklet
Copyright © 2020 by Bibliology® Press.
Weimar, California.

All inquiries should be addressed to:
Bibliology Press
PO Box 783
Weimar, CA 95736
info@sacredsound.studio
www.sacredsound.studio

Executive Editor
Erwin G. Nanasi, DWS

General Editor
Janell Nanasi

**Project Director,
Managing Editor**
Esther B. Nanasi

Editorial Assistants
Natalie Fish
Alexis Hasse
Melissa Osadchuck

Design
Dominique Quinger

ISBN-13: 978-1-954090-00-2

First Edition 2020
Printed in China

Table of Contents

All Scripture is given by inspiration of God, and is profitable
for doctrine, for reproof, for correction, for instruction
in righteousness, that the man of God may be complete,
thoroughly equipped for every good work.
2 Timothy 3:16-17

From the Publishers

The Bibliology Booklet was developed to deepen the reader's personal relationship with God and His Word. It is the supreme hope of the publishers that the reader will experience Jesus Christ personally (Luke 24:27; John 17:3), behold Him consistently (2 Corinthians 3:18), serve Him decidedly (Joshua 24:15) and share Him wholeheartedly (Deuteronomy 6:5-9).

The Publishers of Bibliology®

About the Booklet

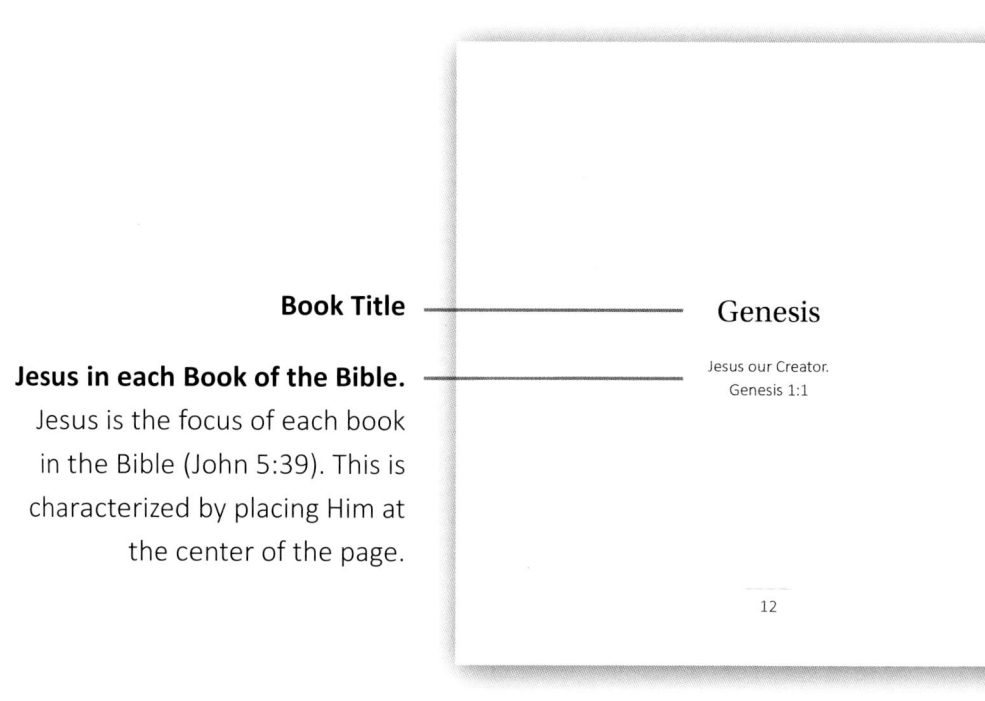

Book Title

Jesus in each Book of the Bible.
Jesus is the focus of each book
in the Bible (John 5:39). This is
characterized by placing Him at
the center of the page.

Genesis

Jesus our Creator.
Genesis 1:1

12

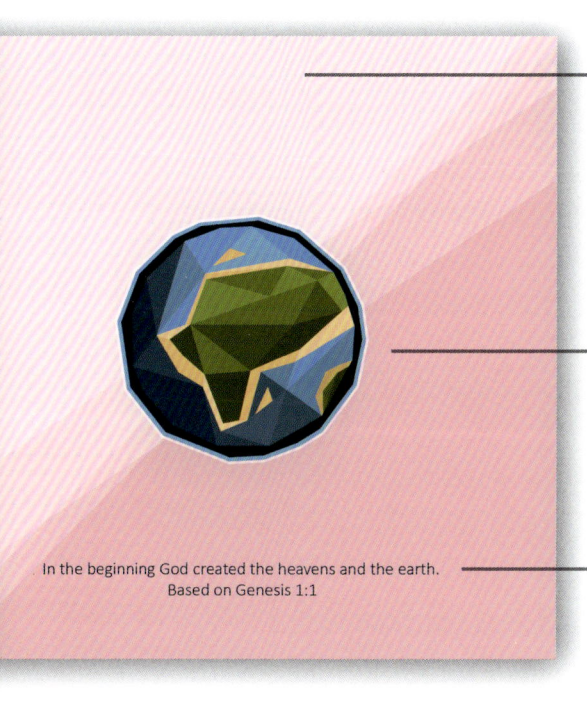

In the beginning God created the heavens and the earth.
Based on Genesis 1:1

Background Colors

The background colors correspond with the eight genres of the Bible.

Original Icon

Each book of the Bible is illustrated by an original icon.

Icon Scripture Reference

Each book of the Bible includes a scriptural reference that inspired the artwork.

The Old Testament

Genesis
Exodus
Leviticus
Numbers
Deuteronomy
Joshua
Judges
Ruth
1 & 2 Samuel
1 & 2 Kings
1 & 2 Chronicles
Ezra
Nehemiah
Esther
Job
Psalms
Proverbs
Ecclesiastes

Song of Songs
Isaiah
Jeremiah
Lamentations
Ezekiel
Daniel
Hosea
Joel
Amos
Obadiah
Jonah
Micah
Nahum
Habakkuk
Zephaniah
Haggai
Zechariah
Malachi

Genesis

Jesus our Creator.
Genesis 1:1

In the beginning God created the heavens and the earth.
Based on Genesis 1:1

Exodus

Jesus our Rock.
Exodus 24:12

The LORD wrote the ten commandments on two tablets of stone.
Based on Exodus 24:12

Leviticus

Jesus our High Priest.
Leviticus 16:4

Moses placed the ephod on Aaron.
Based on Leviticus 8:7

Numbers

Jesus our Provider.
Numbers 11:7-9

The spies carried one cluster of grapes on a pole.
Based on Numbers 13:23

Deuteronomy

Jesus our Reward.
Deuteronomy 28:12

Do not add or take away from the word that the LORD your God commanded.
Based on Deuteronomy 4:2

Joshua

Jesus our Deliverer.
Joshua 6:16

The children of Israel marched around Jericho seven times,
and the priests blew the trumpets.
Based on Joshua 6:15-16

Judges

Jesus our Judge.
Judges 11:27

There was no king in Israel in those days,
and everyone did what was right in their own eyes.
Based on Judges 21:25

Ruth

Jesus our Kinsman Redeemer.
Ruth 4:10

Ruth stayed close by the young women of Boaz
to glean until the end of the harvest.
Based on Ruth 2:23

1 Samuel

Jesus our Strength.
1 Samuel 30:6

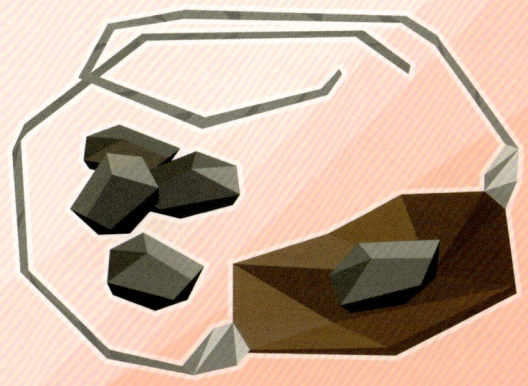

David chose five smooth stones for his sling.
Based on 1 Samuel 17:40

2 Samuel

Jesus our Conviction.
2 Samuel 12:7

Prophet Nathan said to King David, "You are the man!"
Based on 2 Samuel 12:7

1 Kings

Jesus our Assurance.
1 Kings 18:20-40

The fire of the LORD fell and consumed the burnt sacrifice.
Based on 1 Kings 18:38

2 Kings

Jesus our Healer.
2 Kings 20:1-11

The LORD brought the shadow on the sundial ten degrees back.
Based on 2 Kings 20:11

1 Chronicles

Jesus our Temple.
1 Chronicles 28-29

David prayed, "Give my son Solomon a loyal heart to build the temple."
Based on 1 Chronicles 29:19

2 Chronicles

Jesus our King.
2 Chronicles 7:12-18

God hears the prayer of His people.
Based on 2 Chronicles 7:14

Ezra

Jesus our Teacher.
Ezra 7:10

Ezra prepared his heart to seek, do and teach the law of the LORD.
Based on Ezra 7:10

Nehemiah

Jesus our Leader.
Nehemiah 4

Every worker wore his sword while building.
Based on Nehemiah 4:18

Esther

Jesus our Intercessor.
Esther 4:15-17; 5:1-3

King Ahasuerus held out the golden scepter,
and Queen Esther touched the top of it.
Based on Esther 5:2

Job

Jesus our Justification.
Job 13:16; 14:16-17

Job fell to the ground and worshiped anyway.
Based on Job 1:20

Psalms

Jesus our Praise.
Psalm 118:22-23

Praise the LORD with a ten-stringed instrument.
Based on Psalm 33:2

Proverbs

Jesus our Wisdom.
Proverbs 2:6

My son, eat honey because it is good.
Based on Proverbs 24:13

Ecclesiastes

Jesus our Preacher.
Ecclesiastes 1:2; 3:1-13

There is a time for everything.
Based on Ecclesiastes 3:1

Song of Songs

Jesus our Bridegroom.
Song of Songs 8:6-7

Set me as a seal upon your heart and arm.
Based on Song of Songs 8:6

Isaiah

Jesus our Sacrifice.
Isaiah 53

He was led as a lamb to the slaughter.
Based on Isaiah 53:7

Jeremiah

Jesus our Consolation.
Jeremiah 30-31

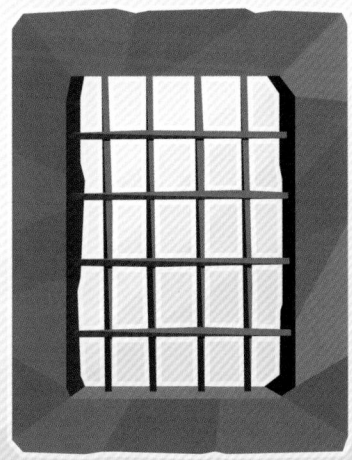

They took prophet Jeremiah and cast him into the dungeon.
Based on Jeremiah 38:6

Lamentations

Jesus our Faithfulness.
Lamentations 3:22-24

How lonely sits the city
That was full of people!
Based on Lamentations 1:1

Ezekiel

Jesus our Life.
Ezekiel 37:1-14

The LORD God gives life to dry bones.
Based on Ezekiel 37:5

Daniel

Jesus our Vision.
Daniel 2:1-49

King Nebuchadnezzar had a dream about a great image.
Based on Daniel 2:31

Hosea

Jesus our Husband.
Hosea 2:14-23

The LORD commanded prophet Hosea to marry a harlot.
Based on Hosea 1:2

Joel

Jesus our Blessing.
Joel 2:18-32

The LORD your God causes the former and latter rain to fall.
Based on Joel 2:23

Amos

Jesus our Shepherd.
Amos 1:1-2; Psalm 23

Prophet Amos was a shepherd.
Based on Amos 1:1

Obadiah

Jesus our Most High.
Obadiah 4, 17

"Though you ascend as high as the eagle,
I will bring you down," says the LORD.
Based on Obadiah 4

Jonah

Jesus our Missionary.
Jonah 3:1-3

The LORD prepared a great fish to swallow Jonah.
Based on Jonah 1:17

Micah

Jesus our Forgiveness.
Micah 7:18-19

God will cast all our sins
Into the depths of the sea.
Based on Micah 7:19

Nahum

Jesus our Stronghold.
Nahum 1:7

The LORD is good,
A stronghold in the day of trouble.
Based on Nahum 1:7

Habakkuk

Jesus our Sacred Place.
Habakkuk 2:20

Let all the earth keep silence before the LORD.
Based on Habakkuk 2:20

Zephaniah

Jesus our Mighty One.
Zephaniah 3:16-17

The LORD your God will rejoice over you with singing.
Based on Zephaniah 3:17

Haggai

Jesus our LORD of Hosts.
Haggai 2:20-23

The Lord said to Zerubbabel,
"I will shake heaven and earth."
Based on Haggai 2:21

Zechariah

Jesus our Anointed One.
Zechariah 4:1-14

Two olive trees stood by the lampstand.
Based on Zechariah 4:3

Malachi

Jesus our Promise Keeper.
Malachi 3:8-10

The LORD of hosts will open the windows of heaven to bless you.
Based on Malachi 3:10

The New Testament

Matthew
Mark
Luke
John
Acts
Romans
1 Corinthians
2 Corinthians
Galatians
Ephesians
Philippians
Colossians
1 Thessalonians
2 Thessalonians

1 Timothy
2 Timothy
Titus
Philemon
Hebrews
James
1 Peter
2 Peter
1 John
2 John
3 John
Jude
Revelation

Matthew

Jesus our King.
Matthew 24:14

The first living creature was like a lion.
Based on Revelation 4:7

Mark

Jesus our Servant.
Mark 10:45

The second living creature was like a calf.
Based on Revelation 4:7

Luke

Jesus our Son of Man.
Luke 10:33

The third living creature had a face like a man.
Based on Revelation 4:7

John

Jesus our God.
John 3:16

The fourth living creature was like a flying eagle.
Based on Revelation 4:7

Acts

Jesus our Power.

Acts 2:1-4

You shall receive power by the Holy Spirit,
and be witnesses to the end of the earth.
Based on Acts 1:8

Romans

Jesus our Grace.
Romans 5:8

Christ died for us while we were still sinners.
Based on Romans 5:8

1 Corinthians

Jesus our More Excellent Way.
1 Corinthians 12:31

Love is a more excellent way.
Based on 1 Corinthians 12:31

2 Corinthians

Jesus our Glorification.
2 Corinthians 3:7-18

By beholding we become changed.
Based on 2 Corinthians 3:18

Galatians

Jesus our Seed.
Galatians 3:16, 19-29

The fruit of the Spirit is love, joy, peace, longsuffering, kindness, goodness, faithfulness, gentleness, and self-control.
Based on Galatians 5:22-23

Ephesians

Jesus our Warrior.
Ephesians 6:10-20

Put on the whole armor of God to withstand the devil.
Based on Ephesians 6:11

Philippians

Jesus our Humility.
Philippians 2:5-11

Let the mind of Jesus Christ be in you.
Based on Philippians 2:5

Colossians

Jesus our Lord.
Colossians 1:9-18

All things were created by and for Him.
Based on Colossians 1:17

1 Thessalonians

Jesus our Resurrection.
1 Thessalonians 4:13-18

The Lord will descend from heaven and we will meet Him in the air.
Based on 1 Thessalonians 4:16

2 Thessalonians

Jesus our Mediator.
2 Thessalonians 2:3-12

That Day will not come unless the falling away comes first,
and the man of sin is revealed.
Based on 2 Thessalonians 2:3-4

1 Timothy

Jesus our Example.
1 Timothy 4:12

Do not neglect what has been given to you by the laying on of hands.
Based on 1 Timothy 4:14

2 Timothy

Jesus our Inspiration.
2 Timothy 3:16-17

All Scripture is given by inspiration of God.
Based on 2 Timothy 3:16-17

Titus

Jesus our Elder.
Titus 1:5

Set things in order and appoint elders in every city.
Based on Titus 1:5

Philemon

Jesus our Ransom.
Philemon 18

If he has wronged you or owes anything, put that on my account.
Based on Philemon 18

Hebrews

Jesus our Hope.
Hebrews 6:19-20

This hope is sure and steadfast.
Based on Hebrews 6:19

James

Jesus our Truth.
James 4:8

Be of one mind.
Based on James 4:8

1 Peter

Jesus our Purity.

1 Peter 1:6-9

Your faith is much more precious than gold.
Based on 1 Peter 1:7

2 Peter

Jesus our Sanctification.
2 Peter 1:5-11

Diligently add to your faith virtue, knowledge, self-control,
perseverance, godliness, brotherly kindness, and love.
Based on 2 Peter 1:5-7

1 John

Jesus our Love.
1 John 4:12-19

God is love.
Based on 1 John 4:16

2 John

Jesus our Joy.
2 John 12

I did not wish to write to you with paper and ink
but hope to see you face to face.
Based on 2 John 12

3 John

Jesus our Health.
3 John 2

Beloved, I pray that you are well.
Based on 3 John 2

Jude

Jesus our Savior.

Jude 20-25

Save others by pulling them out of the fire.
Based on Jude 23

Revelation

Jesus our Everlasting Gospel.
Revelation 14:6-7

Another angel flew in the midst of heaven,
preaching the everlasting gospel to those on the earth.
Based on Revelation 14:6

Resources

For more information, additional resources and feedback visit www.bibliologygame.com.

Bibliology Notecards

OT & NT Bibliology Set

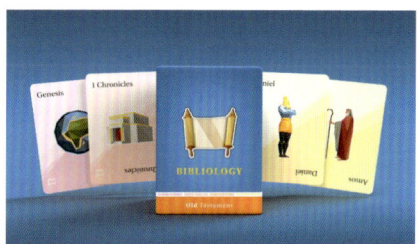

OT Bibliology Set

NT Bibliology Set

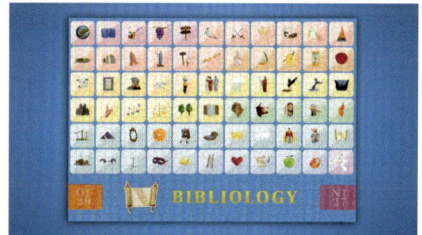

Bibliology Puzzle (1000 Piece)

Bibliology Memory Game